JUN 17 2015

j 811.6 S161c
Chatter, sing, roar,
 buzz :poems about the rain
forest /
Salas, Laura Purdie.

D0617957

WITHDRAWN

WITHDRAWN

Poetry

Chatter, Sing, Roar, Buzz

Poems about the Rain Forest

by Laura Purdie Salas

Capstone press

Mankato, Minnesota

2

Silent Stalker

Jaguar
slinks
through
fronds of
green
walking
stalking
low
unseen

pacing
pathways
crossing
streams

POUNCE!

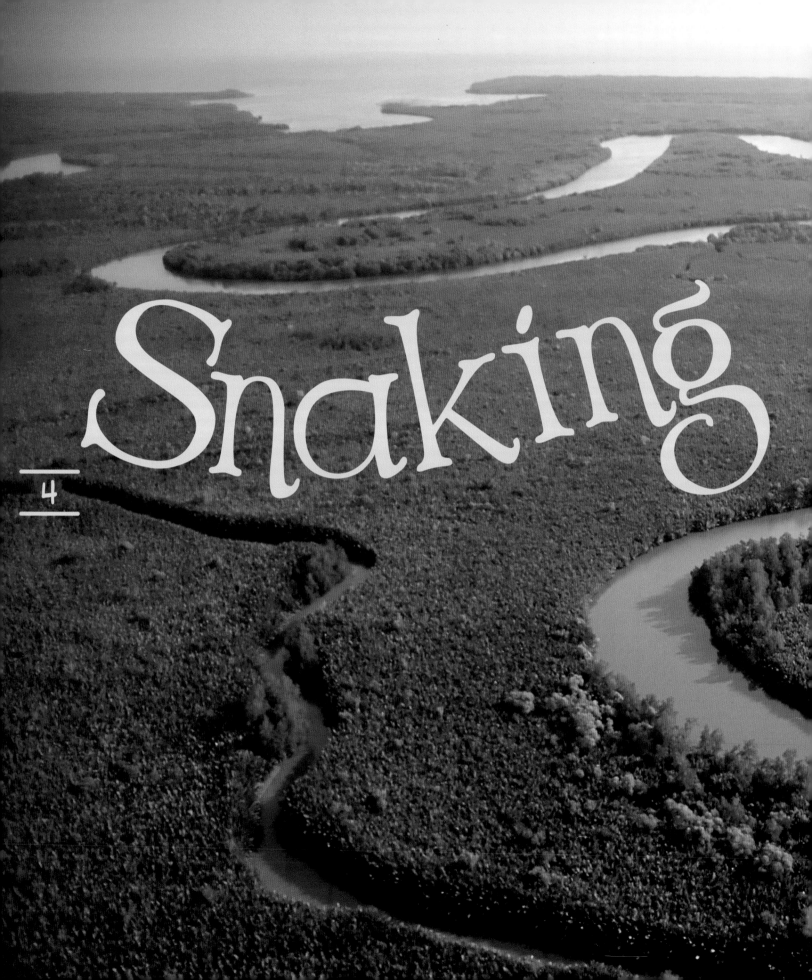

Snaking

Rivers
slither
through
like

snakes
stretching
in sun,
rippling
sleek
muscles

Chores?
What Chores?

my parents groom

    and eat all day

but little chimps

    are made for play

that's me jumping,

    tumbling, springing

soon I'll be

    liana-swinging

A liana is a thick vine that hangs on trees.

Caught up in a moment

Surprised that I'm there

He's giving my camera

a cute, flirty stare

His beard's nice and wiry

His ears aren't too big

He's really quite handsome

. . . for a bearded pig!

Hi There, *Handsome!*

Proud to Be a Leaf-Cutter Ant

You look at me and see small

but my chain-saw jaw slices

leaves into huge pieces

twenty times my weight that I balance

and carry home to my nest

Small can be
powerful!

Slow Thoughts of a Three-Toed Sloth

The forest moves around me
Howler monkeys climb over
Hummingbirds flit around
Even the plants

Shoot up faster than I do

I might live my entire life
On this single embauba tree

But that's ok

A tree makes good company
And I have a lifetime to
Really get to know it

Rain Floats

Mist hangs and hovers

Clouds settle in the forest

Rain floats in mid-air

Deadly Beauty

Bright blue

skin colored like

deep lakes or twilight skies,

but below that skin lies deadly

poison

The Blue Poison Frog's color tells other animals that it is poisonous and not good to eat!

Rain Forest
Parade

Honduran tent bats, which can fit in the palm
of your hand, rest under rain forest leaves.

Two-inch bats
in leafy shade
Teeny-tiny bat
cascade,
Furry cotton ball
parade

Snowballs in the
summer heat
Fuzzy bubbles
mini-feet
Who knew bats
could look so sweet?

A Lemur Mom in Madagascar

I searched all day for ripe papaya

So you could have your snack

I looked for slinky, sneaky snakes

To fight off an attack

You bickered all this afternoon,

I missed our well-worn track

We're finally home; I need to rest —

So please, get off my back!

To the Banana

Thick skin forms
a rain-proof seal
You're a fruit
with great appeal

I pack a lot
of things for lunch
But you're my favorite
of the bunch!

Tender

mother

capybara

bristly fur, gnawing teeth

sharing a juicy stem with her

baby

19

Treetop Scientist

My lab is high among the trees
I scramble up and down with ease
I climb to work, and this is why:
I'm doing science in the sky

Boots are sturdy, helmet's tough
I'm in the field, I'm living rough
I dangle free, enjoy the breeze
Because I'm high among the trees

21

22

Fishing

Feet sunk in mud

Dangling stick in water

Will the Congo River feed him?

Hoping

Mbuti Boy

Clearing the

Rain Forest

25

here

green, lush

growing, reaching, breathing

chattering,   singing,   roaring,   buzzing

slashing, burning, cutting, destroying

brown, barren

gone

One Drop

26

at a Time

Flashing from skies

Splashing in puddles

Dripping off leaftips

Slipping down hills

Rushing in rivers

Gushing toward oceans

Spilling past rocks

Filling up creeks

Streaming in valleys

Steaming the very air

Water creates rain forest creates water

The Language of Poetry

Alliteration — to have the same beginning sound for several words

Couplet — two lines that end with words that rhyme

Rhyme — to have an end sound that is the same as the end sound of another word

Rhythm — the pattern of beats in a poem

Cinquain

A poem with five lines. The first line has two syllables. The second line has four, the third has six, the fourth has eight, and the last line has two syllables. "Tender" (page 19) is an example of a cinquain.

Concrete Poem

A poem in which the words are shaped like the subject of the poem. "Snaking" (page 5) is a concrete poem.

Diamonte

A diamond-shaped poem with seven lines. The top half of the poem describes the first word, and the bottom half of the poem describes the last word. "Clearing the Rain Forest" (page 25) is a diamonte poem.

Free Verse

A poem that does not follow a set pattern or rhythm. It often does not rhyme. "Slow Thoughts of a Three-Toed Sloth" (page 11) is an example of free verse.

Haiku

A short poem that describes a scene in nature. It has five syllables in the first line, seven syllables in the second line, and five syllables in the third line. "Rain Floats" (page 12) is a haiku.

Glossary

barren (BAIR-uhn) — empty

bicker (BIK-ur) — to argue about unimportant things

bristly (BRISS-lee) — short and stiff

capybara (ka-pee-BAYR-uh) — a rain forest rodent

cascade (kass-KADE) — something arranged in a downward pattern

flirty (FLUR-tee) — playful and sweet

flit (FLIT) — to fly quickly from one place to another

frond (FROND) — a large, divided leaf on a plant

groom (GROOM) — to brush and clean an animal's fur

lab (LAB) — a place where a scientist works; lab is short for laboratory

liana (lee-AHN-uh) — a thick vine of the rainforest

lush (LUHSH) — having lots of healthy plants

Mbuti (mm-BOO-tee) — a group of native people that lives in a tropical rain forest in Africa

papaya (puh-PAH-yuh) — a sweet, yellow tropical fruit

slash (SLASH) — to cut

sleek (SLEEK) — smooth and shiny

slink (SLINK) — to move in a slow, smooth way

Read More

Berkes, Marianne. *Over in the Jungle: A Rainforest Rhyme.*
A Sharing Nature with Children Book. Nevada City, Calif.:
Dawn Publications, 2007.

Salas, Laura Purdie. *Rain Forests: Gardens of Green.* Amazing
Science. Minneapolis: Picture Window Books, 2007.

Internet Sites

FactHound offers a safe, fun way to find Internet sites
related to this book. All of the sites on FactHound
have been researched by our staff.

Here's how:

1. Visit *www.facthound.com*

2. Choose your grade level.

3. Type in this book ID **1429617055** for age-appropriate sites.
   You may also browse subjects by clicking on letters, or by
   clicking on pictures and words.

4. Click on the **Fetch It** button.

FactHound will fetch the best sites for you!

Index of Poems

Chores? What Chores?, 6

Clearing the Rain
Forest, 25

Deadly Beauty, 13

Hi There, Handsome!, 7

Lemur Mom in
Madagascar, A, 16

Mbuti Boy, 22

One Drop at a Time, 27

Proud to Be a
Leaf-Cutter Ant, 9

Rain Floats, 12

Rain Forest Parade, 15

Silent Stalker, 3

Slow Thoughts of a
Three-Toed Sloth, 11

Snaking, 5

Tender, 19

To the Banana, 18

Treetop Scientist, 20

A+ Books are published by Capstone Press,
151 Good Counsel Drive, P.O. Box 669, Mankato, Minnesota 56002.
www.capstonepub.com

Copyright © 2009 by Capstone Press, a Capstone imprint. All rights reserved.
No part of this publication may be reproduced in whole or in part, or stored in a
retrieval system, or transmitted in any form or by any means, electronic, mechanical,
photocopying, recording, or otherwise, without written permission of the publisher. For
information regarding permission, write to Capstone Press, 151 Good Counsel Drive,
P.O. Box 669, Dept. R, Mankato, Minnesota 56002.

Printed in the United States of America in North Mankato, Minnesota.
102014
008468R

Library of Congress Cataloging-in-Publication Data
Salas, Laura Purdie.
    Chatter, sing, roar, buzz : poems about the rain forest / by Laura Purdie Salas.
    p. cm. — (A+ books. Poetry)
    Includes bibliographical references and index.
    Summary: "A collection of original, rain forest-themed poetry for children
accompanied by striking photos. The book demonstrates a variety of common poetic
forms and defines poetic devices" — Provided by publisher.
    ISBN-13: 978-1-4296-1705-5
    ISBN-10: 1-4296-1705-5
    1. Rain forests — Juvenile poetry. 2. Children's poetry, American. I. Title.
PS3619.A4256C48 2008
811'.6 — dc22   2008011731

Credits
Jenny Marks, editor; Renée T. Doyle, book designer; Ted Williams, set designer;
    Wanda Winch, photo researcher

Photo Credits
Corbis/Royalty-Free, cover, 1, 28
DigitalVision, 13
Getty Images Inc./National Geographic/Randy Olson, 22–23; Stone/David
    Noton, 12
James P. Rowan, 14–15
Minden Pictures/Claus Meyer, 19; Frans Lanting, 2–3, 4–5, 7, 21; Gerry Ellis,
    10, 24–25; JH Editorial/Cyril Ruoso, 6; Mark Moffett, 8–9
Shutterstock/Ben Heys, 26–27; Eric Gevaert, 16–17; Veronika Trofer, 18

Note to Parents, Teachers, and Librarians
Chatter, Sing, Roar, Buzz: Poems about the Rain Forest uses colorful photographs
and a nonfiction format to introduce children to poetry and life in rain forests.
This book is designed to be read independently by an early reader or to be read
aloud to a pre-reader. The images help early readers and listeners understand
the poems and concepts discussed. The book encourages further learning by
including the following sections: The Language of Poetry, Glossary, Read More,
Internet Sites, and Index of Poems. Early readers may need assistance using
these features.